MW00886189

GO FORTH AND EAT BALLS!

Copyright © 2023. All rights reserved.

Recipe List

January
Freezing My Snowballs Off No-Bake Balls

February
Red Velvet Balls

March
Lemon Blueberry Energy Balls

April
Minty Irish Cream Balls

May
Cherry Chia Energy Balls

June
Key Lime Balls

July
Chewy Popcorn Balls

August
Hard Melon Balls

September
Potato Chip Choco Balls

October
Beer Meatballs

November
Maple Sausage Death Balls

December
Cinnamon Sugar Balls

Bonus: The Classic Cheese Ball

JANUARY

Freezing My Snowballs Off No-Bake Balls

Ingredients:

- ½ cup butter
- 1 cup peanut butter
- ½ cup powdered sugar
- 1 cup graham cracker crumbs
- ¼ cup powdered sugar, for rolling

Instructions:

1. In a large bowl, whisk the butter and peanut butter together until smooth and well combined. If your butter is not soft enough to whisk, warm it up.

2. Add the graham crumbs and powdered sugar and mix until a thick dough is formed. Chill the mixture for about 2 hours.

3. While the mixture is chilling, do the activities on the next two pages.

4. Use a tablespoon to scoop the mixture then roll into a ball. Repeat the process until all of the balls are rolled.

5. Roll each ball generously in powdered sugar.

6. Cover and store in the fridge in an airtight container for up to 7 days.

Things That Can Eat My Balls in January

1. Going back to work again

2. Peak month for treadmill accidents

3. Dropping your keys in the snow

4. _____

5. _____

6. _____

7. _____

8. _____

9. _____

10. _____

January Word Search

```
A B L I Z Z A R D H U W X V U L B U O A
F T N M K D W A Y U G J S B D P S R E E
C E G T O H B W S D C H D F X V E X H C
A S V A A T E U H I O L P K D T G B I A
S E D E R A W V Y U I K P F A D R E B A
G D E N R E F A I O L P J H F T G E E N
U I B E E G R E T Y V B S H I V E R R I
V C D T U A R Q W B J D N G Y Y U C N E
N I R A S L R E E N G Y E F L K S O A H
A C S Y U I N R E L P W T A C T R E T V
B L U R R Y E E N Z F T P S Y B A E E E
H E D R N I M O C W X T I V W A L F H A
V T F U V E X W Z Y B K M B S L S V Y S
E R T B A R U H K N X H K A W R G U J
A A F T V T B K P I K N M B C X S Z R F
U A S D A R E E I K L I W U N H M V G C
A S I B V G U O L O M O B E T E R D A S
V B A L L S G Y H D N D U I N I K P L J
H E G H T W P U S R R P T R P A N P I
Y E Y E J I E L H T F T W L E E S V O A
B D G T K O G I B Y D I S J A N U A R Y
C T J D L L M K G U E O Z I H T D T L U
```

1. January
2. Mittens
3. Shiver
4. Icicle
5. Snowball

6. Blizzard
7. Blue
8. Balls
9. Evergreen
10. Hibernate

FEBRUARY

Red Velvet Balls

Ingredients:

- 1 red velvet cake mix (and the ingredients to make it)
- 1 cup cream cheese frosting
- 24 ounces white chocolate
- Sprinkles for decorations

Instructions:

1. Bake the red velvet cake mix according to the directions on the box.

2. While you are waiting, you can check out the puzzles on the next two pages.

3. Crumble up the cooled cake into a large bowl. Add the frosting and mix it well.

4. If the mixture is too dry to form into balls, add more frosting a spoonful at a time until it takes on a smooth workable consistency.

5. Roll the mixture into 1-inch balls and place on a parchment lined baking sheet. Place in the freezer for about an hour.

6. Melt the white chocolate slowly over a double boiler.

7. Dip the balls in the white chocolate using a toothpick or a fork. Set the balls on parchment paper to harden. If you want to add sprinkles add them right away while the chocolate is still wet.

8. Store in the fridge for a few days.

Things That Can
Eat My Balls in February

1. Presumptuous groundhogs

2. Peak month for bad first dates

3. Accidental texting

4. _____

5. _____

6. _____

7. _____

8. _____

9. _____

10. _____

Only People Who Love Balls Can Finish this Maze

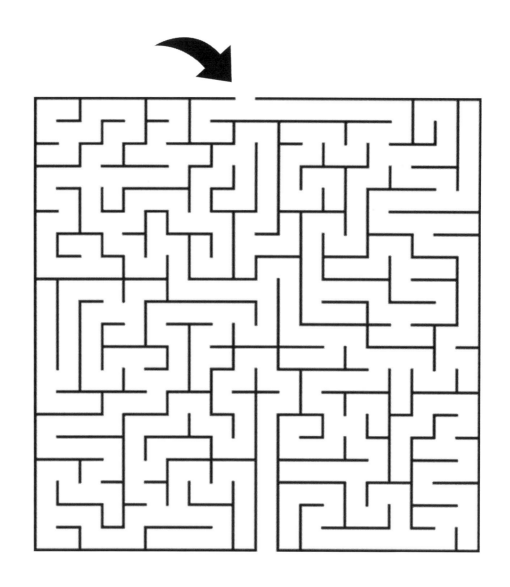

MARCH

Lemon Blueberry Energy Balls

Ingredients:

- 1½ cups cashews
- ½ cup unsweetened shredded coconut & additional for rolling
- ½ cup dried blueberries
- ¾ cup dates, pitted and roughly chopped
- 1-2 tablespoons fresh lemon juice
- 1 teaspoon lemon zest
- ½ teaspoon vanilla extract
- Pinch of fine sea salt

Instructions:

1. Blend cashews and coconut in a food processor until they become a coarse meal.

2. Add blueberries, dates, lemon zest, lemon juice, vanilla extract and salt. Process until the mixture forms a rough dough that will hold together in balls.

3. Form into 1-inch balls. Roll the balls in additional coconut. Store in an airtight container in the fridge for up to a week.

Things That Can
Eat My Balls in March

1. Daylight savings time

2. Peak month for vasectomies

3. Your balls are still cold

4. _____

5. _____

6. _____

7. _____

8. _____

9. _____

10. _____

Who Eats Green Balls?

Tom, Meera, Jan, Levar and Sam are all friends who love balls. At their monthly ball party, each person eats a different color of balls, and each eats a different number of balls.

- Jan ate 3 balls

- Someone ate 1 pink ball, and it was not Meera

- Levar likes yellow balls

- Tom ate more than 3 blue balls

- Someone ate 2 red balls

- Levar ate more balls than anyone.

- Jan hates red balls.

- Meera ate fewer than 4 balls

- Sam ate either pink balls or red balls.

Who ate the green balls?

APRIL

Minty Irish Cream Balls

Ingredients:

- 1 package of mint Oreos
- 1 (8 oz.) package of cream cheese
- 3 Tbsp Irish Cream liqueur
- 1 (12 oz.) semi-sweet chocolate baking bar
- Sprinkles

Instructions:

1. Line two baking sheets with parchment paper.

2. Pulse cookies until finely crushed. Mix with cream cheese and Irish Cream.

3. Shape into 1-inch balls and place in freezer for about 30 minutes.

4. While the mixture is chilling, do the activities on the next two pages.

5. Melt chocolate. Use a fork to dip each ball and place on lined baking sheets. Top with sprinkles.

6. Cool the balls in refrigerator until chocolate is set.

7. Store in the fridge in an airtight container for up to 7 days.

Things That Can Eat My Balls in April

1. Taxes

2. Peak month for shipwrecks

3. Forgetting to celebrate National Richter Scale day again

4. _____

5. _____

6. _____

7. _____

8. _____

9. _____

10. _____

Invert the Ball Pyramid

Ten delicious balls are arranged in a pyramid. Turn the pyramid upside down by moving only three balls.

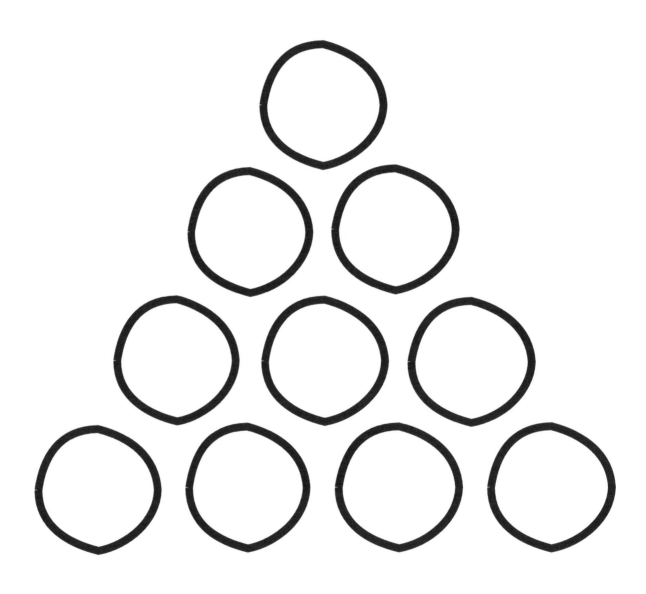

MAY

Cherry Chia Energy Balls

Ingredients:

- ½ cup dried cherries, chopped
- ¼ cup chocolate chips
- ¾ cup rolled oats
- ½ cup unsweetened coconut
- ¼ cup chia seeds
- ¾ cup nut butter (peanut or almond)
- ¼ cup maple syrup

Instructions:

1. Mix all ingredients together.
2. Scoop up tablespoonfuls of the mixture and shape into balls with your hands.
3. Store in an airtight container in the fridge for about a week.
4. Do the puzzles on the next two pages with all your new energy.

Things That Can Eat My Balls in May

1. Eurovision song contest

2. Peak month for hay fever

3. Large swarms of bees

4. _____

5. _____

6. _____

7. _____

8. _____

9. _____

10. _____

Cut-Out Ball Dominoes!

JUNE

Key Lime Balls

Ingredients:

- 1 package (8 ounces) cream cheese
- 1 can (14½ ounces) sweetened condensed milk
- 3 tablespoons lime juice
- 3½ cups graham cracker crumbs
- ½ cup confectioners' sugar

Instructions:

1. Mix first four ingredients together
2. Shape into 1 tablespoon balls and roll in confectioners' sugar
3. Refrigerate for 30 minutes.
4. Complete the activities on the next two pages while you wait.
5. Store in an airtight container in the fridge for about a week.

Things That Can Eat My Balls in June

1. Warm weather mania

2. Peak month for cancelled flights

3. Not knowing what to do with your life

4. _____

5. _____

6. _____

7. _____

8. _____

9. _____

10. _____

Solve the Ball Wheel

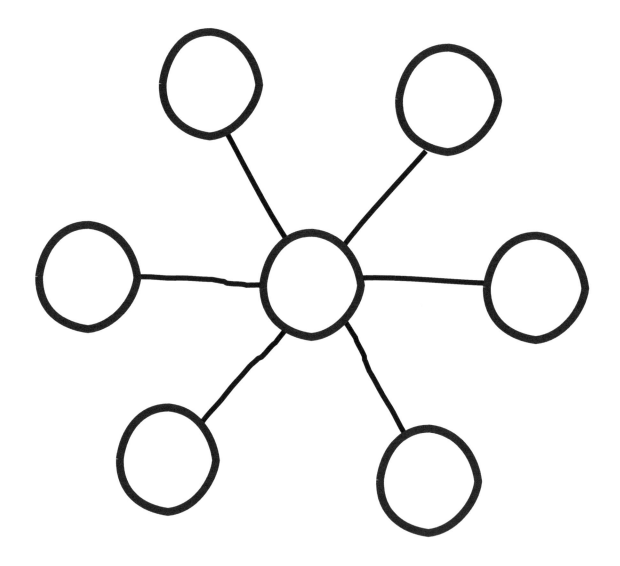

Seven delicious balls are arranged in a wheel. Label each ball with a number from one to seven. Make each of the three spokes in the wheel equal 10.

JULY

Chewy Popcorn Balls

Ingredients:

- 1 package (10 ounces) mini marshmallows
- ¼ cup butter
- 1 tablespoon water
- 1 package (10 ounces) Jello gelatin, any flavour
- 12 cups popcorn

Instructions:

1. Melt butter in a big pot and add marshmallows, water and gelatin. Stir until melted and blended.

2. Add popcorn and mix.

3. Butter hands and shape into balls, setting each ball on waxed paper when done.

4. Store in an airtight container. Eat soon, while completing the activities on the next two pages.

Things That Can Eat My Balls in July

1. Fireworks and canine freak-outs

2. Peak month for divorces

3. Sunburns

4. _____

5. _____

6. _____

7. _____

8. _____

9. _____

10. _____

July Word Search

```
A B R I L Z A F D H U W X V U L B U O A
F T N M K D W A Y U G J S U M M E R E E
C E G T O H B M S D C H D F X V E X J C
A S V A A T E O O I O L P K D T G B I A
S F D E R A W S Y J I K P F H D R E B A
G I E N R E F Q I O I P J T F T G E E N
U R B E E G R U T Y V T N H J V E R R I
V E D T U A R I W B U E O G U Y U C N L
N W R A S L R T E N V Y E F L K S O A A
A O S Y U I N O E E P W T A I T R E T V
B R U Y R Y B E S N Z F T P U Y B A E I
H K D R N I M O C W X T I V S A L F H T
V S F U V E X W Z Y B K M B S L S V Y S
E R T B A R U H U K N X H K A W R G U E
A A F T E T B K P I N M B C X S Z R F A
U A S D A R E E I K L I W U N H M V E C
A S I B V G U O L O M O B E T E R R A S
V B A L K S G Y H D N D U I N I T P L J
H E G U H T W P U J U L Y T R I A N P I
Y E Y E J I E L H T F T W L V E S V O A
B D G M A R S H M A L L O W S N N A Y B
C A M P F I R E G U E O L I H T D T L U
```

1. July
2. Julius
3. Seventh
4. Fireworks
5. Festival
6. Summer
7. Campfire
8. Marshmallows
9. Mosquito
10. Mojito

AUGUST

Hard Melon Balls

Ingredients:

- A mix of watermelon, cantaloupe and honeydew melons
- 1¼ cup pear juice
- 1 cup vodka
- 4 tablespoons sugar
- Mint leaves

Instructions:

1. Use a melon baller to scoop out a lot of melon balls. Put them in a bowl.

2. Add pear juice, vodka, sugar and mint to the bowl and stir.

3. Cover the bowl and refrigerate for about an hour. Do the puzzles on the next two pages while you wait.

4. Stir the balls.

5. Refrigerate for another hour and serve.

Things That Can Eat My Balls in August

1. Back to school sale anxiety

2. Peak month for homeless kittens

3. Questionable poetry readings

4. _____

5. _____

6. _____

7. _____

8. _____

9. _____

10. _____

Get to the Balls!

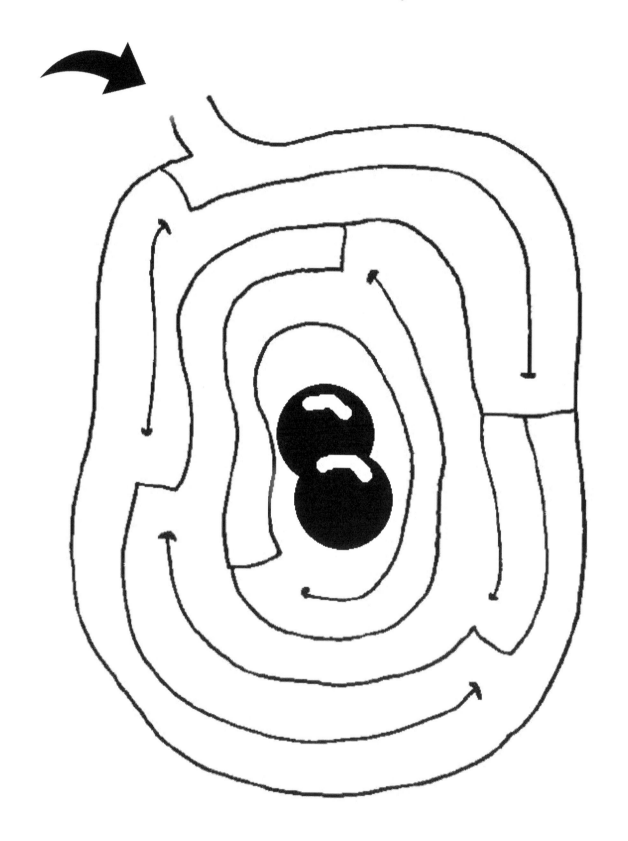

SEPTEMBER

Potato Chip Choco Balls

Ingredients:

- ⅓ cup peanut butter
- ½ cup powdered sugar
- 4 tablespoons almond flour
- 4 tablespoons crushed potato chips, plus extra for topping
- 6 oz bittersweet chocolate

Instructions:

1. Mix peanut butter, sugar, flour and chips together in a bowl.
2. Roll into balls and place on parchment in a tray or baking sheet.
3. Freeze for 15 minutes.
4. Melt the chocolate.
5. Dip balls in chocolate and return to parchment.
6. Dust with extra chips
7. Allow to harden while you do the exercises on the next two pages.

Things That Can Eat My Balls in September

1. Chlorophyll withdrawal headaches

2. Peak month for new backpack smell

3. Your brother will never repay the money he owes you

4. _____

5. _____

6. _____

7. _____

8. _____

9. _____

10. _____

Sorting the Salty Balls

You are applying for your dream job at the Salty Balls Co. packing factory. But you arrive to find everyone in a tizzy.

The labelling machine has gone haywire and is sticking the wrong label on every box of balls!

"If you can label the boxes correctly, without wasting any balls, you'll have a job here for life!" says the boss.

There are three boxes in front of you. One contains salty balls, one contains sweet balls, and one contains a mix of salty and sweet. The only way to tell them apart is by taste.

Can you label all three boxes correctly by tasting only one ball?

OCTOBER

Beer Meatballs

Ingredients:

- 2 pounds of ground meat (any combo of beef, pork or lamb)
- ⅓ cup breadcrumbs
- 4 ounces of amber ale
- 2 large eggs
- 1 medium onion, grated
- 2 tablespoons Italian seasoning
- 1 tablespoon salt
- 1 teaspoon black pepper
- ½ teaspoon garlic powder

Instructions:

1. Set oven to 375.
2. Combine the meats in a large bowl.
3. Beat egg in a small bowl and add beer, onion, salt and spices. Pour over the meat.
4. Add breadcrumbs to bowl and mix.
5. Form mixture into golf-ball sized balls and place on a baking sheet.
6. Bake 25 minutes or until internal temperature of 165 degrees is reached.
7. Do puzzles on the next two pages while you wait. Serve hot.

Things That Can Eat My Balls in October

1. Realizing that Halloween isn't as good as it used to be

2. Peak month for stock market crashes

3. Forgetting about the frozen pizza you put in the oven

4. _____

5. _____

6. _____

7. _____

8. _____

9. _____

10. _____

Connect the Balls

Without lifting your pen, draw through all the balls.

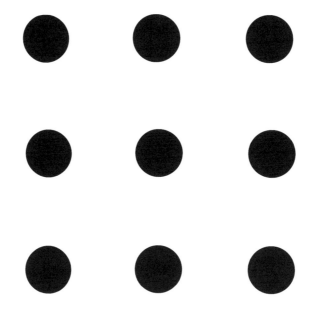

Beginner: use 4 straight lines

Advanced: use 3 straight lines

NOVEMBER

Maple Sausage Death Balls

Ingredients:

- 1 pound breakfast sausage (uncooked)
- 1 (8 oz) package of cream cheese, softened
- 1 cup shredded cheddar cheese
- 1¼ cups Bisquick mix
- ⅓ cup maple syrup

Instructions:

1. Set oven to 400.
2. Combine all ingredients in a large mixing bowl.
3. Line and lightly grease a baking sheet.
4. Form ping-pong ball sized balls and place on sheet.
5. Bake 25 minutes or until browned and internal temperature of 165.
6. Do the exercises on the next two pages while balls are baking.
7. Serve. Try not to die of bliss.

Things That Can Eat My Balls in November

1. The dark and ominous vibe

2. Peak month for magnetic field fluctuations

3. Your pet racoon moving out for good this time

4. _____

5. _____

6. _____

7. _____

8. _____

9. _____

10. _____

Math Can't Bust My Balls

DECEMBER

Cinnamon Sugar Balls

Ingredients:

- 4 cups of vegetable or canola oil
- 1 can refrigerated pizza crust dough
- 1 cup shredded cheddar cheese
- ¼ cup sugar
- 1 teaspoon cinnamon

Instructions:

1. Heat oil to 350 in deep heavy saucepan.

2. Remove dough from can but do not unroll. Cut the dough into 12 equal pieces.

3. Mix sugar and cinnamon together.

4. Roll each piece of dough into a ball and cook in oil for 30 seconds.

5. Use metal slotted spoon to remove balls to the sugar mixture and coat.

6. Do the exercises on the next two pages while you eat all the tasty warm balls. Do not share.

Things That Can
Eat My Balls in December

1. Everything is too shiny

2. Peak month for respiratory illnesses

3. Fruitcake

4. _____

5. _____

6. _____

7. _____

8. _____

9. _____

10. _____

Find a Pair Of Balls

The Classic Cheese Ball

Ingredients:

- 3 (8 oz) packages of cream cheese, softened
- 1 tablespoon Worcestershire sauce
- 1 tablespoon hot pepper sauce
- 1 pound shredded cheddar cheese
- 1 garlic clove, minced
- 1 cup finely chopped pecans
- finely chopped fresh parsley (optional)

Instructions:

1. Blend cream cheese, Worcestershire sauce, hot sauce and garlic in a food processor or with a mixer.

2. Add cheddar cheese and blend until small pieces remain.

3. Shape into two balls and wrap in plastic wrap. It don't have to be perfect.

4. Chill in freezer or fridge until hard, reshape balls if desired.

5. Roll in pecans and parsley (if using).

6. Serve immediately or re-wrap and store in fridge until ready to serve.

Well, my ball-loving afficionados, as you've probably gathered, I'm not exactly your traditional cookbook author. I don't get my kicks from fussy hors d'oeuvres or painstakingly complex patisseries. No, my friends, I revel in the simple, spherical joy that is ball-shaped food. It's in the cheeky side-glances when you tell your friends what you're making, the stifled laughter when you shape your mixture into soft little globes, and the pure, unadulterated joy when you take that first, mouthwatering bite.

I hope you've enjoyed this little book, even if it made your life more nutty, messy, and sticky at times (sound familiar?). Remember folks, balls aren't just a dessert. They're an experience to be savored.

Best wishes to you and yours,

Cherry Jewel

The Solutions

January Word Search

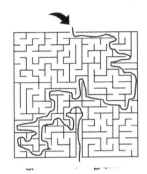

July Word Search

Only People Who Love Balls Can Finish this Maze

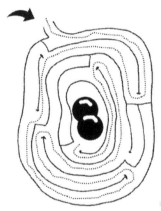

Who Likes Green Balls?

Name	Ball Color	Number Eaten
Tom	Blue	4
Leslie	Red	2
Rick	Yellow	5
Sam	Pink	1
Jan	Green	3

Jan ate the green balls.

Invert the Ball Pyramid

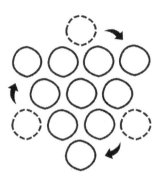

Solve the Ball Wheel

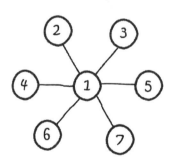

Sorting the Salty Balls

Since each box of balls is labelled incorrectly, taste one ball from the mixed box. If it is salty, you know that the box labelled sweet must contain the mixed balls, and the box labelled salty must be mixed.

Find a Pair of Balls

Connect the Balls

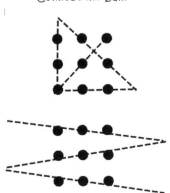

Math Can't Bust My Balls

$$5 + 1 + 8 = 14$$
$$15 - 2 - 6 = 7$$
$$4 + 7 + 3 = 14$$
$$16 - 4 - 4 = 8$$

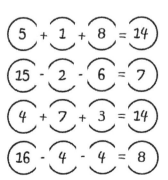

Made in United States
Orlando, FL
02 December 2024

54807004R00030